Pawfriendly Landscapes™

How to share the turf when your "backyard belongs to Barney"

by Elizabeth Bublitz

– Dedication –

This book is for everyone who protects animals and is a voice for them.

It's also for my sister, Caroline; my parents; Helen; Brenda; Nora; Beth & Gary; Tracy; Christine; my long-lost cousin, Judi; Warren; my Grandpa Keirstead; all my landscape crews; and to my wonderful clients who made this book possible by being so generous and letting me "experiment" with their yards!

Last, but certainly not least, this book is for all my pets, past and present (there are too many to name individually) who have shown me the most pure form of love!

– Acknowledgements –

Lori Cavanaugh, Photographer/Artist
Thanks for all your beautiful photos.

Ann M. Diaz, MA
Thanks for being a great editor and keeping me motivated; you're the acorn to this project!

Good Samaritan Pet Agency
Thanks for doing so much work for pets.

Heather Green, Studio Bella LLC
Thanks for the cover layout.

Nicci Hyatt, Realtor - www.110Realty.com
Thanks for being such an amazing client and for the picture of Oscar.

John Kuepper, Creator of Cat Man Do
Thanks for all your work with my book and for protecting the welfare of cats!

Bob & Kathy Lamerand
Thanks for being such great clients and for sharing your photos for our cover.

Kelley Sands, Graphic Designer
Thanks for always helping with all our printing needs, our logo, and for reworking the cover.

Laurie Schilz, Illustrator
Thanks for being so easy to work with.

Judith H. Spurling, D.V.M.
I'm glad we got to do this project together. Thanks for always being my mentor!

Mary Walewski, Buy the Book Marketing
Thanks for holding me together during this process!

CMC Coloredge
Thank you for creating a pet friendly edging

Thanks to various organizations who have let me lecture about pet-friendly yards: Associated Landscape Contractors of Colorado, Colorado Free University, Denver Botanical Gardens, and the Denver Dumb Friends League.

A PORTION OF THE PROCEEDS
WILL BENEFIT GOOD SAMARITAN PET AGENCY, DENVER.

- Table of Contents -

– Introduction –

"Our new puppy ate our yard."
"Help! Our terrier cut himself on the edging."
"My cat wants 'outside.' How do I keep her safe?"

Do any of these scenarios sound familiar to you? Have you found yourself wondering how your pets and your yard can harmoniously co-exist? The very existence of this book should be an indicator to you that 1) your pet is not uniquely "destructive," and 2) you are not alone in your frustration and your desire to create a pawfriendly yard.

As a professional landscaper and devoted animal-lover, I am so delighted to have found some solutions to your "backyard belongs to Barney" issues—and I'm even more excited to share my expertise with you. There is nothing more rewarding than someone who says, "We did not relinquish our dog because of our new pawfriendly landscape, which lets him have his freedom and allows us to enjoy, too!" Now you, too, can create the best backyard for both you and your beloved pets!

Whether you have a 10-pound terrier, several 120-pound labs, or a clan of inquisitive kitties, these ideas are applicable and as easy to follow as the commands "sit, stay, roll over"! (Well, OK, if you can get a *cat* to "sit, stay, and roll over," you need to write a book of your own!) You'll learn the basics of having a beautiful backyard that makes *everyone* happy and safe in any climate. You will also learn about how to protect your pets from toxic houseplants and other hazards, how to keep your pups from "digging to China," and more great tips on how to keep your landscape living...and livable. This approach to pawfriendly backyard space is inexpensive, attractive, and best of all, easy to install.

There is hope, folks. And I'm here to share with you my ideas, success stories, and how-to advice on creating outdoor spaces with your pet's safety and well-being in mind. Come along with me as we create the perfect backyard for you, and most importantly, your critters!

***

Meet the Pawfriendly Landscape specialists and colleagues that will guide you through this book:

Elizabeth Bublitz
Pawfriendly Landscapes™
Golden, Colorado

Pawfriendly Landscapes™ is the pioneer in creating yards that are pet-friendly! As its owner, I've been blessed with wonderful clientele who have allowed me and my team of specialists to create the perfect yards for them as well as their pets. Their stories, situations, and frustrations were each unique but had common threads—all of which I have drawn from to find solutions that will work for others, just like you. (I'll share some of their stories here, too. But the names will be changed to protect the cuddly and innocent.)

Judith Spurling, DVM
Parker, Colorado

Just like people, animals need guidance on how to best live in their spaces. Generally their digging and chewing is an indication of other issues, not a sign of bad genes! I'm thrilled to share with you advice from my friend, the highly regarded veterinarian Dr. Judith Spurling. Watch for Dr. Spurling's **TRAINING TIPS** boxes throughout the book.

Barney
fun-loving doggie
Anywhere, USA

It only seems fair that my Barney has a chance to share his wisdom. I've learned a great deal about pawfriendly yards from observing him and his dear playmate, Otis, and adapting my landscaping techniques to what they tried to tell and show me. You can learn about your pets' needs by watching them, and by heeding some of Barney's **TAILWAGGIN' TIPS**. After all, it's their yard, too!

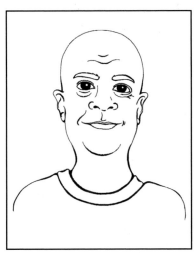

John Kuepper
Cat-Man-Do
Denver, Colorado

As you may have guessed, most of the pet-scaping ideas in this book pertain to canines. It just seems we never get the call, "My cat ate my backyard." (But who knows? I should never say "never"!) But cats have needs too, so I have called upon the expertise of my friend John. He has a wealth of experience when it comes to protecting our feline friends so they can roam outside, protected from the dangers in a secure environment.

***

- Landscape Terminology -

Before getting started, I want to familiarize you with words that will be used throughout this book. It might be helpful for you to skim through this page early on, then come back to it when you stumble across a word that needs to be defined.

Amended soils are soils that have been altered by the addition of manure (such as sheep or cow manure, which acts as a nutrient) or spaghum peat moss (which acts as an aerator, breaking down clay-like soil). Some bulk stores sell a mixture of manure and peat by the ton or yard. Soil amendments should be added to topsoil or backfill when installing plants.

Annuals are all-season blooming plants that grow for only one season, generally from spring until fall. Since they bloom all season, they can be an attractive focal point to any garden, including perennial or shrub gardens. Gardeners love that annuals bloom all season and that they can redesign their gardens every year with different annuals.

Bedlines are the edging or borders that create a separate garden or section in a yard.

Beds are free-form gardens that can be viewed from all sides.

Biennials are plants that produce only foliage in their first year and flowers in their second year of growth. The flower produces seed that begins a two-year cycle for the following spring.

Berms are free-form beds that have an elevation to them or that are surrounded by a large scale of grass, rock, or wood mulch. A berm is much like an "island" in the middle of a yard. It breaks up a large scale very nicely by adding different textures and elevation.

Border gardens are gardens with a structure (such as a building) or a form (such as a hedge) behind them. They are viewed from only one side.

Cobble rock is small, medium, or large round river rock. It is very awkward to walk on for humans as well as for pets, so we use it to prevent dogs from walking in gardens. The size of a pet is a factor in determining the size of cobble needed. For instance, a Yorkie terrier would be deterred by a 3-foot-wide small cobble bed, but a mastiff would be deterred by a 4- to 5-foot-wide large cobble bed. Cobble rock is very beautiful rock mulch when used as an accent. Because gaps tend to appear due to the different sizes of cobble, top-dress (or sprinkle) 1.5-inch river rock on cobble to fill it in and soften its appearance.

Edging is the barrier that divides different material in yards. It prevents one material from migrating to another material.

Flagstone or pavers are used to create walkways or patios. Flagstone is either irregular (like puzzle pieces) or cut in various sizes like 12x12-inch or 12x18-inch. There are numerous types of tumbled pavers: brick, concrete, earth stone, exposed aggregate, and others.

Landscape fabric (WeedShield and Typar are common brands) is a breathable cloth that is installed under rock mulch. Make certain it is breathable so it allows moisture to penetrate it and does not suffocate plants. Some fabrics require use of pins for installation. Landscape fabric helps you keep maintenance to a minimum, though there is no guarantee that grass and weeds will not grow in areas with fabric. Many times the wind or birds will relocate seeds to the mulched areas and they will sprout on top of the fabric.

Perennials are flowers that come back year after year. They do not like to grow with landscape fabric around them, so be sure to plant these in a garden with wood mulch (since WeedShield is never used with wood mulch).

Rip rap is large chunks of granite (usually 6 to 18 inches wide) used on slopes for erosion controls. Rip rap is gray and rugged, with very irregular and sharp edges. Due to its sharp edges, homeowners and professional landscapers tend to prefer cobble for deterring dogs from walking in gardens.

Rock mulch includes various forms of rock that are installed in shrub and tree gardens. Rock mulch typically comes in .75-inch or 1.5-inch size. It is generally used with a landscape fabric, such as WeedShield or Typar.

Textured plants are plants that are not smooth-leafed; they have a texture to them. Examples include lamb's ear, Russian sage, creeping evergreens, and thistle.

Winter features are plants that are interesting year-round. Some plants keep their color, such as barberries and evergreens; others keep an interesting shape or form, such as ornamental grasses.

Wood mulch includes various forms of shredded, chipped or processed wood that is used for shrub, flower, or tree gardens. Landscape fabric is not used with wood mulch because this mulch's purpose is to decay and work its way into the soil like an aerator. If fabric is installed, the wood mulch will blow off. We use wood mulch with perennials because perennials do not like fabric around them. It does not kill them, but it restricts their growth since, unlike trees and shrubs, perennials spread as they grow. There is more maintenance with wood mulch because (1) you must always add more as it weathers, and (2) weeding is more common because there is no fabric to prevent weeds from growing.

Chapter 1: You Are Not Alone!

You can try to reason with your Backyard Barney all you want—others in similar situations have tried. But the fact is, it's just not gonna work! Dogs'll be dogs, folks. Perhaps it will help you to know that you are not alone...and that your Backyard Barney isn't being unruly or disrespectful.

Here's just one example of a "true story" situation you might relate to...along with our remedy.

Rescuing the rescuer
Ken rescued and fostered golden retrievers—three or four of them at a time. Unfortunately, Ken's yard was literally demolished due the size and high energy of these lovable dogs. To make matters worse, he lived on a green belt, so walkers constantly came by and "triggered" his dogs to run back and forth. Ken tried to fix the situation by reseeding the area and installing a temporary fence to allow the grass to "heal." However, the dogs simply started to run along the temporary fence and destroyed the sod outside the temporary fence.

Our remedy: Ken was trying to fight the inevitable. Instead of trying to save the grass, a new bedline needed to be created for the retrievers. We suggested he remove the grass along the fence—usually a 3-foot-wide path is comfortable for one or two dogs, but in his situation where he'd have four at one time, we created a 4-foot-path—and install edging and a walkway. We installed pea gravel for them to walk on since pea gravel is very comfortable to dogs. (In our later chapters, we'll get into more detail about mulches for dog paths.) We used a patio edging since the dogs created so much foot traffic with their size and their energy. (See chapter 2 on "Ouchless Edging.")

You'll find lots of stories like Ken's—and yours—throughout this book. These **"From the Trenches"** situations are what we good-heartedly call "learning from others' mistakes." I mean really...we're only human!

Chapter 2: Ouchless Edging is a Great Start

One of the most important features in landscape is edging. Why is it so important? Because every landscape has to have it! When I'm called out to a client's home to redesign their landscape, I always know that edging will be used. Edging must be used in landscaping whenever there is a transition, and in every yard there will be a transition. It's inevitable—which is why we are going to examine many different types of it! A transition is when we put two or three different materials next to each other. For instance, when rock mulch is installed, there has to be something that prevents it from migrating to other materials, such as grass or wood mulch. This "something" is called edging. It acts like a dam between the two different areas.

Choosing the right type of edging is very important and must be carefully considered because dogs can easily cut their paws on edging while playing in "their" yards! By the way, I've also seen many humans cut themselves while installing or transporting steel edging, so this discussion on safe edging applies to us humans, too. A cut paw (which, for some reason, usually happens after regular veterinarian hours!) is a horrifying experience for the dog and dog owner. Just ask Dr. Spurling (see sidebar). However, it is so nice to know all of this can be avoided by using the right type of edging!

Edging *is* necessary, but it doesn't have to be a necessary evil! Again, it is simply a division of some sort, which is used as a transition in your yard, and there are many different solutions. In our pet-friendly landscaping experience, we have used many different types of edging with great success. In fact, you might be surprised at what you have lying around your house or garage that you can use as edging!

Edging commonly causes lacerations to the web between the pads on the paw. The pads can also be lacerated or nearly cut off. Since the pads are very vascular, bleeding is common and can be severe, especially if arteries are cut.

This experience doesn't necessarily stop at the veterinarian's office. The long-term effects of severed tendons include the inability to move the toes. The toes and nails may be pointing upward instead of holding on to the ground.

One type of edging that we will *not* be considering is steel edging, even if it comes with a "safety" cap. I put quotes around the word *safety* because the cap has a tendency to weather and pop off—regardless of how many edging pins are used—thus exposing the sharp, knife-like edge. Even the sides of steel edging are sharp. No person or animal should ever be subjected to a nasty cut from steel black edging! Most people use steel black edging because it is cheap and very easy to install, but as Mom always said, "You get what you pay for!" However, steel edging *can* be used in the front yard if there is not a lot of foot traffic. This will help you minimize costs in one area so the money can be put in the backyard where it is necessary. If you're comfortable having steel edging in the front, then one word of caution: If either your children or your pets are in the front yard, minimize their activity and be very careful!

TAILWAGGIN' TIPS

Here's a money-saving tip from ol' Barney: It might cost a little more and take a bit more time to install, but safer edging will pay off in the long run. You save yourself some money (and mental anguish for you and me both!) by not paying extra vet bills when you use a safer edging in your yard.

Before You Install Edging

First you must determine where your edge line is and define it. You can mark your proposed edge line using spray paint, a garden hose (if you have one long enough), or flour, which is nontoxic. You should also set out the edging next to your proposed line to make sure you have enough to cover your linear footage. In my example I will use spray paint since it's what "we pros" use every day. Having a bright color is best, especially if you're going to paint on grass. And be sure to use inversion paint. This is the best paint since you'll be holding the can upside down. Trust me, I've wasted many hours trying to unclog a regular can of spray paint while creating edge lines! (See? I'm willing to share not only my triumphs but also my disasters!)

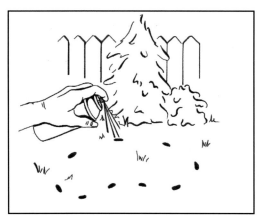

It's best to "dot out" your desired garden bedline. The closer the dots are drawn, the easier it is to see the line when you step back and "connect the dots" in your mind. Using dots on your proposed bed line is more practical than drawing out full lines; you might find yourself with so many lines that they'll all blend together and you won't remember which one you prefer! Keeping everything simple is key.

Simply dot out the proposed site, stand back and literally connect the dots using your 20/20 vision. Of course, it's also much easier to smudge out dots with your foot than eliminating lines, especially in areas where grass exists. When you're finally happy with the formation of the dots, go ahead and revert to your childhood and connect those dots. Stand back and see the beginning of your new masterpiece in your own backyard!

Your next step will be to remove enough grass to create a small, snug trench to fit your edging. Then you'll be ready to install the edging according to the manufacturer's instructions.

If you're installing brick or any edging that has significant width (pavers, flagstone, interlocking blocks, timbers), you'll need to install landscape fabric before laying the edging. Landscape fabric prevents weeds from growing up through your edger. It's sold by the square foot, so be sure to calculate before you head out the door. You'll also need to make sure your trench is level, since brick is laid into a trench and not pounded into the ground like some other edging. If it's not level, your new edge line will look like a moving inchworm! It can also buckle and not serve its purpose of preventing one material from migrating into another material. So keep in mind regardless of the surface, whether it's in sod or soil, the trench must be level.

Various Forms of Edging

Your local landscape supply store will have a variety of options for edging. Here are some considerations.

TAILWAGGIN' TIPS

Maybe you're removing your existing black steel edging and starting over with a newly shaped bedline, just for me! Wow! I feel loved.

BRICKS, PAVERS, AND BLOCKS: There are many styles of bricks, pavers, and blocks available at landscape supply stores. But before you go out and spend money, look around your own home first. Many new homes (and a few older ones) have bricks left over from the builder, usually stashed away in the garage. Do not throw these away!

FROM THE TRENCHES

Steve's shortcut snafu

Steve installed a brick edger along his perennial bed but did not remove the existing grass — he simply placed the brick on the grass hoping it would suffocate the grass. In other words, he wanted to reduce his work load and not remove the grass. However, he created more of a problem in the long run because the sod simply grew between the crevices of the brick and along the back of the brick so it went into his garden. He was constantly fighting the grass by weeding every weekend. He couldn't enjoy his garden at all due to this problem.

Our remedy: To install any type of hardscape (flagstone, strip stone, brick, etc.) you must remove the existing sod, and then grade the area to make it level. Then you must install landscape fabric and then place the brick on it. This not only eliminates the grass problem so you can enjoy your garden but also your brick will be level and not bumpy. Keep in mind, if the brick has three holes in it, like many of them do, then you must use a landscape fabric under it to prevent grass from growing through the holes.

First of all, brick is almost impossible to match. (So you'll be glad you saved it some day when you need it for an addition or repair to your house.) Use leftover brick in the yard for edging or to build a planter, and you'll have a perfect and inexpensive match to your house. If you don't have enough to do all your edging, you might try mixing styles together to create a pattern or choose another type of edging altogether.

Second, and more importantly, brick has no sharp edges so it will not hurt your Backyard Barney's paws. Dogs can also run on it (if it's installed near their runway) and it stands up beautifully to foot traffic from pets and humans alike.

Third, it is easy to install. You will have a beautiful, safe backyard in no time. A few things to remember: It can be more difficult to create beautiful contour lines with brick unless you own or rent a brick saw (demolition saw). This will increase your cost of labor. Also, if your bedline is on a hill, you'll want to insert a few edging or landscape pins in front of the brick so it does not roll out of its trench as it weathers. You'll simply pound the pins about three inches into the ground so they're not noticeable; only the brick and Mother Nature will know the pins are there.

CMC COLOREDGE EDGING: Created in Colorado, CMC is a safe metal edging system that provides a viable alternative to the current metal products offered and, at the same time, enhances any landscaping scheme. This edging is very desirable for many reasons!

◆ Safety: The edging has a rounded edge at the top. Because it has an interlocking system, the rounded edges carry all the way across the span of the edging, eliminating those sharp edges so common in current metal products. This removes the concern of children or pets scraping themselves, causing unnecessary injury.

◆ Continuity: The interlocking system provides a continuous line from one end to the other. No breaks and no overlaps are required. The edging comes in 10-foot sections with color-coordinated pins to secure it to the ground.

◆ Uniformity: There are currently four colors to choose from: green, sandstone, terra cotta, and black, as well as galvanized metal and copper. You can match your edging with your landscape; for example, terra cotta can be used next to wood mulch, and sandstone is a perfect accessory for your stone displays.

◆ Durability: The edging and pins that CMC offers are derivatives of the products offered by metal roofing contractors. Metal roofs are manufactured to last 25 to 30 years without rusting or fading. The same holds true for CMC Coloredge. The colors are baked in the metal and are rust resistant. They are intended to stand up to virtually any weather conditions without losing their appeal. The metal is 18 gauge, and because of the interlocking design, it actually has a sturdiness equivalent to 12 gauge. This ensures that the edging will remain straight and will not collapse like many of the other metal and plastic edging products now being offered. The pins are a double-sided 16 gauge, with two points of entry into the ground, further adding to the strength and durability of the system.

Another perk to this edging is that the interlocking design reduces installation time. And CMC provides pre-formed corners that allow for easier installation of runs that require 90-degree turns or less. It's simple—just lay out your path and slide the pieces together.

Since Coloredge is attractive, there is no need to "hide" it. You'll actually want it to show up in your landscaping scheme.

PATIO EDGING OR PAVER EDGING: When installing a patio or hardscape, it's best to either use steel edging (which is a big no-no with dogs!) or patio or paver edging, since these were created to reinforce patios. Since there is so much weight against the edging of a patio (it has sand, road base, breeze, etc.) most of the other pet-friendly edging won't hold patios in place. Thankfully, patio edging is pet-friendly and does the trick! It is easy to install and usually comes in 7-foot strips with pins.

STRIPSTONE: Stripstone is beautiful. But more importantly, it is pet-friendly! It usually comes in buff or red and is 4 to 8 inches wide. When you lay out your proposed edge line, you must measure your linear feet and order the stripstone accordingly (it's available by the ton). One ton of 4-inch stripstone covers 65 square feet; whereas one ton of 8-inch stripstone covers 21 square feet. When you call your local supplier, be sure to have your linear footage available so they can convert it. It can be installed exactly like the brick edging.

TIMBERS: Timbers come in 8-foot lengths and are generally treated green or brown. Timbers are great to use near a driveway because they don't pop tires like steel edging has been known to do. However, along a shrub garden, timbers can be awkward because they do not make a beautiful contour line like other edgings. You'll have a lot of cuts to do if you do want a contour line, and the timbers will have to be installed like the brick edging. Then, you'll have to pound rebar into them to hold them in place. They are attractive and pet-friendly, but they have a few negatives: they're a lot of work to install, they do not create beautiful contour lines, and they have a shelf life. That's right—they rot! Your Backyard Barney will enjoy the timbers, but do be sure to pound the rebar in so it's not exposed (ouch!).

STEEL ROLL-TOP EDGING: No, your eyes are not deceiving you! You do see the word *steel*, but it's very pet-friendly in this situation. Roll-top edging has the look of steel edging and it also needs pins, but it does not require a safety cap. Unlike steel edging, roll-top edging's "cap" is rolled over the top of the edging so it can never pop off and hurt your pet's paws. When planning, know that steel roll-top edging is generally sold in increments of 10 feet. To install this edging, it's best to first create a narrow 4-inch-deep trench (similar to how you'd prepare for brick edging, but this requires no landscape fabric). Once the trench is complete, simply install the roll-top edging by pounding it in, usually with the bottom of a pick. Like stone edging, this requires more labor, but in the long run, your Backyard Barney will be very thankful.

WEEPY EDGING: This edging is much like the roll-top except it has holes in it—like a cheese grater—and lets water run through it. That's why they call it weepy:

It's as if the edging is crying! Most edgers can act like a dam and hold water back; however, weepy edging lets it escape. It's great for areas around your foundation, where you don't want water to settle. It's also great for low spots because it allows water to move through it (forward) rather than allowing it to puddle, dam up, wash away neighboring mulches, or create erosion! But most importantly—you guessed it!—it's pet-friendly. Weepy edging is also sold in 10-foot increments and needs pins, so know your linear footage. One negative, since it has holes, it also can allow grass or certain mulches to migrate, which kind of defeats the purpose of edging.

BLACK JACK EDGING: This edging can be tricky to install because it doesn't give you the clean contour lines that weepy or roll-top edging can give you. You must also trench to install this edging and use edging pins in the trench to secure it. Unlike other safe edging, it usually comes in 20-foot increments and corners need to be installed, which can be a hassle. Also on the down side, Black Jack edging doesn't weather as nicely through the winter and it tends to pop up. However, it is a good pet-friendly option.

***

Edging is one of the most important steps in your new pet-friendly, pawfriendly backyard! Armed with this advice, you can define your bedlines and then head to your local bulk material landscape store to discuss the options with a salesperson. Be sure to ask about all the materials you'll need for a successful installation; they know their stuff. You and your Backyard Barney will be grateful once your yard has some defined structure and you've created a safe space to play!

Chapter 3: "Diggers" and Other Escape Artists

In this chapter, we'll address common reasons dogs dig and examples for fixing the problem. One of the most common calls I get is this: "My dog has destroyed my backyard because he is digging everywhere!"

Many veterinarians agree that many dogs dig because they're bored and they simply need more to do! If you suspect this might be the case, try walking your Backyard Barney more or playing ball or catch with him in his backyard. It's amazing how easy dogs are to please because they're actually more interested in pleasing you. When you structure their lives and teach them new tricks or train them to do the commands you want them to, they are happier because they are pleasing you. Becoming frustrated and angry with your dog does not help matters whatsoever; you must keep in mind, he really wants to make you happy, so communication between you and him is key. Cats, on the other hand, are a whole different animal—they may want to please you, but they'll never let you know that!

If you play with your Backyard Barney enough and have ruled out that he is digging because he is just bored, then digging might be due to something else: maybe he is burying his bone, digging from habit, checking out something that smells good (perhaps manure was installed), curious about water trickling (such as a sprinkler head or near a downspout), or just has an urge to dig and dig. The good news is that there are many simple, economical solutions that only you and your Backyard Barney will know about because they're not conspicuous at all!

Here are some solutions:

Install chicken wire

Chicken wire is the most common solution because it is cheap and easy to install. However, the best reason to use chicken wire is nobody has to know it's there. We keep it under the mulch to prevent your Backyard Barney from digging. One word of caution: Chicken wire cannot be used to prevent your little guy from digging in the sod; but don't worry, we'll offer solutions for that too.

TAILWAGGIN' TIPS

If I'm digging to China, maybe it's because I really do want to see a real Shar Pei! I've probably tried three or four places. If you leave just one or two of those tunnels open for me—the ones in inconspicuous areas are fine, if that's what makes you happy—then I'll likely be satisfied and not start all over again elsewhere.

Chicken wire should be installed after the landscape fabric and before the rock mulch, or directly under the wood mulch. (Note: Do not use fabric with wood mulch; it will simply blow or slide off the cloth. Keep in mind that wood mulch ultimately decomposes and works its way back into the soil, acting as an aerator. Installing fabric is counterproductive to the purpose.)

TRAINING TIPS: Dr. Spurling

Choosing mulch with caution

Chewing sticks and mulch is common, especially in the younger puppies. If they chew up a lot, it can cause obstructions in the stomach or intestines. If they swallow large pieces it may block the GI tract or actually choke the pet. Splinters can lodge between the teeth or on the roof of the mouth, which will cause the dog to paw at his face trying to loosen the stick. If pieces get into the stomach, they may cause vomiting or irritation and the dog may lose weight or not eat well. Sometimes pieces pass and cause bloody stools or diarrhea.

On the other hand, some dogs will eat gravel or rocks and become obstructed.

If either or both are the case for your Backyard Barney, then consider concrete or pavers. If the mulch is not for their bathroom area, then install cobble; dogs cannot carry cobble around due to its size. These are all easy to clean and can be hosed regularly.

If your Barney doesn't eat wood mulch, use it for his bathroom area; it neutralizes the smell.

After grading the area and choosing the best mulch for you and your pets, it's time to secure chicken wire onto the landscape fabric or into the ground with edging or landscape fabric pins. Then install mulch over the top. When your Backyard Barney begins to dig, his paws will hit the chicken wire and he will dislike the texture. Please note that if you need to cut the wire to size it, the edges will be very sharp—as sharp as edging. This could seriously hurt your dog when he digs on it. To prevent this, fold over the newly cut edge

and secure it with an edging or landscape fabric pin. Be sure to check the safety of the chicken wire by scratching at it as if you were imitating a dog. The last thing you want is to turn a "dig to China" into a trip to the vet's emergency room.

To create a "Fort Knox," install a large rock mulch such as 6- to 12-inch cobble or rip rap on top of the chicken wire. Dogs (and humans!) dislike walking on large rock; it's very awkward for them, so they tend to stay off of it. Cobble is the more attractive choice for homeowners. If your Backyard Barney is petite, you can use small to medium cobble. A 2-foot-wide cobble accent should be plenty. If your dog is medium size, then I recommend using medium to large cobble and creating a 2- to 3-foot-wide cobble accent. If he's a big fellow, I recommend using large cobble to create a 3- to 4-foot cobble accent, depending on the size of the area. In this case, you can soften the look by tossing some 1.5-inch rock mulch over the top.

Chicken wire can also be used to prevent your pet from being an escape artist. There is nothing more frightening than looking into your backyard and seeing that your dog has dug his way out by going under the fence! Dr. Spurling says the most common accident is an animal being hit by a car. Thankfully, this is also preventable. When a dog digs under a fence to escape, we fasten chicken wire to the fence with staples, wire, or nails (depending on the material of the fence)

FROM THE TRENCHES

McGruff's crime

Dana installed edging along her fence to prevent her dog, McGruff, from digging out. Not only did this not prevent McGruff from digging out, but her edging continued to pop up and shift as it weathered.

Our remedy: Do not install edging at the bottom of your fence—this does not deter dogs from digging. The main problem is that it doesn't stay in place; all it does is shift and rub against your fence. It also pops up from the ground and will expose its sharp edges, which will hurt your dog. To keep McGruff in his yard, we stapled chicken wire about three-fourths of the way down on the fence (or about a foot up from the ground), then brought it down to meet the ground to form an "L" shape, and then secured it to the ground with edge pins. In addition to this remedy, to create a Fort Knox-effect, we added cobble and fabric on top of the chicken wire. This is not only pretty, but it deters dogs from digging since they don't like the feel of it. It's also good for drainage and maintenance; since fence lines are always drainage points, the water will follow the cobble. Also, since you've created a new cobble bedline, you won't have to pull weeds, mow, or irrigate up to your fence—it's a perfect solution for many issues!

Along those same lines...if you have chain link or a three rail fence with some kind of wire, simply install edging pins at the bottom of the chain link or wire to prevent your Barney from escaping.

and secure the chicken wire into the ground using edging or fabric pins. Installing cobble on top of the chicken wire also prevents your dog from digging. One of my clients had two huskies who continued to escape by digging under the fence. We first installed cobble, but this did not deter them from escaping. However, after installing chicken wire under the cobble, the doggies remained in their backyard and their owner could live in peace knowing her dogs were out of danger. So remember, chicken wire can be a lifesaver to your pet!

Try textured plants and decorative lattice

Another solution for doggies digging in flower or shrub gardens is to plant textured plants. This is very attractive, and nobody but you and your lovable critters needs to know why you've chosen these plants! Whatever your climate, there are many beautiful plants to choose from. If you live in a cold climate, for example, winter-interest plants with thorns or texture are in abundant supply. These are not only great deterrents to dogs but are very pleasing in your landscape. When ol' Barney starts to dig or romp in the garden and gets poked a few times, it will deter him from entering that particular garden. Creeping or low-growing textured plants such as creeping junipers, pyracantha, rose carpet, or barberry prevent dogs from digging. Again, if you want to create a "Fort Knox" garden to prevent digging, incorporate a few textured/thorny plants with your chicken wire and mulch for an inconspicuous yet effective design.

While some dogs escape by digging under a fence, others escape by climbing fences. Thorny plants can help prevent this. Try planting climbing roses and securing lattice horizontally using 2x2s to keep your pets from playing Houdini. When a dog scales a fence and runs into lattice, he'll generally give up. Thank goodness!

Utility boxes are often located next to fences, and some dogs use them as launching pads to jump over fences. To prevent this from happening, we use lattice or a gate around the box. *When doing this yourself, remember to leave a 3- to 5-foot clearance when digging, since you're working around utilities; be sure to call your utility company to locate all underground utilities before you dig! They'll mark your utilities for free and they'll do it in 24 hours.

There are many attractive choices to prevent your Backyard Barney from climbing and escaping. Adding some attractive climbing roses to your lattice or fence would be nice, or use textured shrubs to hide the utility box and fence. However, keep in mind, the utility company has the legal right to cut back any of your plants/lattice for access to the boxes, if necessary.

Attractive thorny or textured plants include:

Barberry (year-round foliage plant with thorns; red, yellow, or green)

Creeping evergreens (year-round foliage plant; blue variety turns to purple in winter, also green varieties)

Roses (climbing or rose carpets)

Pyracantha – (interesting orange berries in the winter)

Place a boulder

Boulders are also an effective deterrent for digging dogs. And here's a bonus: if your Backyard Barney has already dug a hole, he's already created a place for an attractive boulder! You'll want a hole for the boulder to rest in so that it doesn't look like a head stone.

There is a true art in installing boulders, so choose one with the best face. Ask for a professional to install it; if your pups haven't dug out enough dirt for the boulder, the professional will be able to do so. A dog, of course, cannot dig through a boulder; however, your Backyard Barney might get the clever idea to dig *around* it, so chicken wire or cobble might need to be installed around the base of the boulder.

Boulders are attractive winter features. They can be appreciated during every season and in any type of garden.

Use mothballs

Many people call to tell me their little rascal is digging in the sod or grass. Since chicken wire, boulders, and thorny plants are useful for garden areas but not for grass or sod, you'll need another solution. We recommend using mothballs where your digging dude is acting like a mole.

Mothballs also keep your Backyard Barney from going into certain gardens and help prevent the neighbor's cat from using your gardens or backyard as a litter box. Sometimes dogs stay away from the areas immediately, but often it takes a few weeks for them to avoid the area.

However, some dogs actually eat mothballs, which are toxic and can make them very sick. Be sure your Barney does not turn them into a new play toy! If this is the case, reseed the area and install a temporary fence, or install a deciduous tree where he's digging (not an evergreen—their needles kill all plant material under them and they do not like a lot of water; they'll get the same amount of water the sod does and this will stress them out!)

Reseed the sod

If there are multiple patches of grass that have been dug up, consider fencing off the areas with cheap, easy-to-install construction fence and reseeding. The fences are available at most big hardware stores. If your dog respects the fence, then you can reseed the area and keep him off of it.

To reseed, try broadcasting grass seed by hand and putting peat moss over the top. We do not put soil on top of the seeds because soil is dense and can suffocate or stress the existing grass blades, creating a weed problem or killing good grass. Instead, simply top-dress the seed with peat moss (it's not heavy and loamy) and water in the seeds. Watering grass seed can be tricky—you want to water it well but not so much that you wash the seed away. So be sure to keep an eye on the area for the growth of new blades, while also keeping your "diggers" at bay.

Many people opt for this when there is a large area they are reseeding. It's amazing how the cheapest fence can keep your Backyard Barney off the germinating grass, so don't overlook this simple option. However, once the grass is established, he may go back to his old tendencies, so you may have to use mothballs.

Redesign the area

Sometimes the best solution to a dug-up area of grass is to simply remove the patch of grass altogether and replace it with a shrub garden, especially if this is Barney's go-to place. This solution works best if the problem area is near an existing shrub garden and if you can incorporate this new area into it.

TAILWAGGIN' TIPS

"I love sprinkers!"

I'm not chewing on the sprinklers to get a time-out. No way! When I hear and see that water shooting out, I wanna play! If you program the sprinklers to turn on when I'm not outside, I'll probably forget they're there. And I really don't like mothballs or walking on cobble, so those are some other hints. Just be careful to not install anything that may prevent the sprinkler head from popping up and doing its job. Then no one will be happy! Arf!

Chapter 4: For Dogs Only / Designs by Barney

Perhaps you're interested in creating a separate space in your yard for your Backyard Barney. You may even have a doggie door from the house or garage to a fenced-in area of the yard for Barney to come and go as he pleases (kind of like having separate in-law quarters). Creating a dog area is often an ideal way to provide a nice, safe sanctuary for your pets to play, apart from other people-only areas. The idea is not to make the dog feel "banned" from the rest of the yard, but to give him an area to be happy and feel comfortable. And, if makes you a little less anxious about the rest of your yard, then everyone's a winner.

Here's the key: *Let your dog train you.* Where does he or she like to run? Is there one general area he usually "does his business?" Does she always hang out under a particular shade tree? Before you make any design decisions, really watch your pets; you'll be surprised at how much they tell you!

When planning your dog area, you'll also want to consider environmental factors. Shelter from the sun and the wind is mandatory; north- or east-facing property is best-suited. If the area you have available gets more sun, be sure to provide access to a cool area, such as a pet door into your house or garage, or provide a shade cloth for your dog area.

TAILWAGGIN' TIPS

My dear friend, this is important: I need access to water at all times. You can find those handy automatic waterers at pet stores. Oh, thank you, thank you! Wag, wag. Slobber, slobber.

You have many options when it comes to creating a special area for your pets. Keep in mind that all you may really need are ways to discourage your Backyard Barney from getting into flower gardens or burrowing under fences, with creative use of cobble and chicken wire, for example. (See Chapters 2 and 3.) Creating an area for Barney to "do his business" is likely to cure many of the problems you're having with your luscious green lawn and yes, you can train a dog to use a certain area (not quite as easily as cats and litter boxes, but along those lines). Alternatively, you could fence off an entire section of your yard or just enough for a dog run. Here are more details to get you started.

Doggie-Doo Areas:

When I'm measuring a yard for a client, I almost always hear the apology, "Watch out, I didn't clean up the dog poop." I never mind this situation because actually the dog is showing me where he eliminates; by respecting those areas (and the fact that, well, a dog's gotta go somewhere!) I have found that we can discretely incorporate "doggie areas" into landscape designs.

> No plants are immune to animal urine or feces; therefore, instead of replacing plants that your Barney lifts his leg on, simply install an attractive container or statue in the same area.

If your dogs are using lots of places to eliminate, try to narrow it down to only two places or so for them to use as a bathroom. (See the tips on Patch-Training Your Dog in this chapter.) Incorporate these bathroom areas as far away as possible from patios or other entertainment areas.

TRAINING TIPS: Dr. Spurling

Minimizing "Lawn Burn"

There really are no "miracle" solutions to prevent urine burns on your lawn. Some specific diets can reduce the burning of the lawn but, in reality, the lawn is burned by excess fertilization from the nitrogen in the urine. (And these types of dog food should not be fed to growing puppies since they are a limited protein diet.) Watering immediately after the dog urinates will dilute the concentration and prevent burning.

Also keep in mind that Backyard "Betty" will leave urine burns in the grass more so than Barney will. So if you own a female dog, be sure to hose down the grassy area to prevent burns.

Patch-training a dog to urinate in specific spots works best. Be sure to reward your pet with high praises for using the designated area.

Myth: "If you bury your dog's feces, it will prevent him from entering that area." This may work but it may not. It may even attract him to defecate there.

TRAINING TIPS: Dr. Spurling

Patch-Training Your Dog
(Note: This is easiest if done when you first get the new dog or puppy.)

1. Use a leash.
2. If necessary, pick up your dog and put him down where you want him to be, rather than doing a yank-and-drag on the leash.
3. First thing in the morning and last thing at night, as well as multiple times during the day, take the pup out to the place you want him to go.
4. Just stand there! Do not move your feet. If the dog goes to the end of the leash, jerk it back gently and quickly, but then release the leash so it is hanging down again. The release of pressure is the reward.
5. Wait only about 5 minutes for the dog to eliminate (usually urine is first, then defecation). As the dog is eliminating, use your secret word, such as "hurry up" or "go potty." Don't use "good boy" or "good girl," because if you say that phrase in the house, the dog will go in the house.
6. If no results, take the dog back in the house, but do not let him loose in the house. If you have had the dog for a while, he may not like to eliminate in front of you since you yelled at him when he went in the house. So he will try to hide "it" from you by running into the other room, behind the refrigerator, under the piano, anywhere you will not see it. Doggy psychology...
7. In 10 to 20 minutes, or after you feed the dog, take him outside again.
8. The dog must stay on a leash, in a cage, or with you. If you take your eyes off the dog, he will go in the wrong place.
9. If you see the dog going in the wrong place, take the several paper towels you have stored in your pocket for this purpose, place them under the dog to collect "it," and pick up the dog and run outside. Then put the dog down where you want him to go.
10. You only have 3 seconds to say "no" to the dog so he knows it is *the place* he is not to go, not the act itself. (They really do have to go!)
11. If he is "guilty looking" when you come home, it's not because he knows he did something wrong. He *does* know that these crazy humans do a very strange yelling and screaming dance when they find "it."
12. If your dog doesn't make you know when he has to go out, either by barking or whining, hang a bell on the doorknob on a cord so he can bump it with his nose when he goes to the door. Let him bump it whenever you go out and want the dog to go out. Open the door as soon as he bumps it and makes the noise—alerting you that he needs to go.
13. This needs to be continued until the dog goes when you say. You will find that the training pays off not only at home but also if you take your dog on a trip; he or she will go on command.
14. Have your dog eliminate before you play with him—urine first, then wait if you know he needs to defecate, using the same phrase ("hurry up") multiple times as he is going. After he is done, *then* say "good dog!" and pet and play. After both jobs are done (in the patch that *you* picked for him to go) then have playtime together.
15. After he consistently goes with you standing by him on a leash, you can tell him to go when he first goes out and you'll only have to clean one place, and you won't have circles where the grass is burned!

In most of my landscape designs, I incorporate the area that the dog is using into the landscape design. It's best to create beautiful contour lines for their doggie area; contour lines always make the yard more interesting. These areas can be quite attractive; screened with lattice and climbing vines/roses or year round plants and winter features such as dogwoods or evergreens.

Some people use cat litter, pea gravel, or river rock. Wood mulch works well because it neutralizes the smell. If your dog eats both wood and rock mulch, consider using pavers. Sand is not recommended because it gets in doggie paws and gets tracked into the house.

If training your dog to use one or two areas is not a viable option, you might just have to periodically re-patch your sod.

Dog-Run Do's and Don'ts

Most dogs love to run. As a homeowner, it might appear to you that your Backyard Barney's goal in running back and forth is to systematically pound out a path in the grass to ruin your lovely lawn. Dr. Spurling says it's much more simple than that: Your dog is simply being a dog! He's happy in his yard and wants to "play" with the neighbors, passers-by, and other nearby dogs or critters. We see the most wear and tear on yards when a dog lives next to a greenbelt or has neighbor dogs who entice him to run back and forth.

The really great news is that creating a dog run, or "runway," is one of the easiest pawfriendly solutions to install. And, runways can be a very attractive addition to your landscape. Here are some tips:

- According to Dr. Spurling, "a dog run should be at least as wide as the dog is long and at least twice that long." Most runs are about 3-feet wide; lengths vary based on available space.

- Consider using pavers or concrete for the surface. Some dogs eat or chew wood mulch, and rock mulch can be difficult to pick up droppings from if your dog eliminates on this area. (And, in particularly humid climates, parasites live in crevices and dirt.) Very active dogs are more likely to scatter the mulch as they dash around.

- If you do choose rock mulch for this area, then choose a variety that is comfortable to walk on, such as river rock or pea gravel. The size of the rock should correspond to the size of your dog or dogs—from pea gravel for smaller dogs to $\frac{3}{4}$-inch to $1\frac{1}{2}$-inch for larger dogs. Pea gravel tends to migrate with larger dogs, so it's very important to consider your dog's size. Also consider the type of foot traffic—for example, small terriers have more energy than Mastiffs, so they are more likely to kick up a lighter-weight mulch.

- Do not use landscape fabric underneath mulch in a dog-run area or any space specially designed for Backyard Barney. The fabric will absorb dog-waste odor and cannot be cleaned off. Instead, add about 3 or 4 inches of gravel first, and then cover it with rock. The purpose of the fabric is to deter grass and weeds from growing; the foot traffic, extra rock mulch, and dog urine will serve this purpose.

- Be sure your dog area is not on a steep slope. A slope allows the rock mulch to collect at the bottom over time, leaving an exposed surface above. Not only will your Backyard Barney be left with exposed dirt to rest and play on, but you'll also have an uneven area that will collect rain water...and bugs. Ick.

- Steer clear of installing bee-attracting plants like bluebeard or blue mist spirea, Russian sage, lavender and lilacs (when they're in bloom). Every plant that blooms attracts bees, so keep that in mind when installing plants around your Backyard Barney's dog area!

- Dogs can learn to climb up chain-link fences, so a top to the run may be necessary. I have seen a beagle tear open a chain link fence from the pole at the botton, enough to get out. They may also break their teeth.

- Remember, any time you create a new type of surface area or bedline, you'll need edging for the transition. Refer to Chapter 2 for details on selecting and installing pet-friendly edging. If you'll be using landscape fabric under your edging, you will want to trim it back so that the fabric is not under your rock mulch.

- As with any landscape project, sharing the task with some of your 2-legged buddies is always easier. Who have you helped move lately? Whose daughter have you purchased 72-dozen Girl Scout cookies from?

> Putting large pots or raised beds in a garden will give your dogs something to lift their legs on so they don't kill plants anymore or trample through a garden.
>
> If lots of plants are installed into a garden, dogs tend to stay out of the bed. This is primarily because dogs do not have good depth perception, so they see large plantings as obstacles. However, the trick is to get the plants established. This is where cobble rock mulch or a temporary fence would help.

Chapter 5: Protection From Hazards

Like small children, our pets count on us to consider potentially hazardous situations in and around the home, and to take measures to prevent these things from happening, including careful plant selection. In this chapter, we'll discuss those measures along with some suggested remedies for emergency situations. We must point out, however, that nothing takes the place of calling your primary veterinarian or animal emergency center or the Poison Control Center: 1-800-222-1222.

Sliced paw on edging:
One of the most important steps you can take in your landscape design is to use pawfriendly edging. Chapter 2 is full of information about recommended edging and installation techniques for the safety of your pets.

These types of cuts can be quite serious and always require your veterinarian's attention. Once you notice the cut paw, wrap it in gauze or a towel and contact your veterinarian immediately.

If you haven't already done so, take a close look at the edging you currently have in your yard and take the necessary steps to ensure safety, even if that means replacing your existing edging. This will save you and your Backyard Barney a dramatic afternoon in the emergency room. Plus, replacing edging is much less draining—emotionally and financially—than a cut paw on your beloved pet.

Natural outdoor hazards and remedies

Bee Stings: Ouch! Pets don't like bee, hornet, or wasp stings any more than people do. Not only are they unpleasant but the pain can go on for quite a while. If your Barney has been stung, it's best to remove the stinger by scraping it with a credit card—do not tweeze it out. You can also apply an anti-itching cream (such as calamine or ammonia) using a cotton ball. Packing the affected area with ice will also reduce the swelling. Like humans, pets can go into an anaphylactic reaction: wheezing, trembling, chills, vomiting, diarrhea, collapse. Contact your veterinarian immediately if he shows any of these signs or if it is his first bee sting.

Cocoa Bean Mulch: Many of my clients have wanted to use this mulch because it smells good (like chocolate!), it's easy to install, and potentially lasts longer than wood mulch. However, I always dissuade them because it has chocolate and that is a toxin to pets!

The toxin is theobromine, which is similar to caffeine and has similar effects: ie, stimulation even to seizures. The heart muscle may be affected with tachycardia (beating more rapidly than normal) and irregular beats (arrythmia). Death can occur within 6 to 24 hours with ingestion of large amounts suddenly, or over several days from cardiac failure if ingested over several days. The signs (or symptoms) are nervousness and excitement, tremors, seizures, panting, and loss of bladder control. Coma and death can ensue. No specific antidotes are known, but supportive treatments with IV medication to control tremors or seizures and medications to slow the heart can be administered. The toxic dose is related to the size of the dog.

If your pet were to eat cocoa bean mulch, you would want to induce vomiting with hydrogen peroxide (3%) and take him to your veterinarian as soon as possible.

Skunk Odor: My dogs seem to only get sprayed by a skunk at 1 o'clock in the morning! And then of course they rub and rub on every piece of furniture, trying to get that stench off of themselves. If you don't have one of the specially formulated skunk shampoos on hand, you might try one of these possible remedies, some given to me by my clients. (Be sure to protect their eyes when you try these).

1. Tomato juice or vinegar bath

2. Inexpensive shampoo, like Suave or Prell

3. Massengill Douche: Apply it to your dog's coat and let it set in for a couple hours before washing it off. Vinegar is the ingredient that deactivates the

smell, so the longer it sets, the better. Even though our instincts tell us to wash our dogs, water always activates the stench, so it's best to let the vinegar set on your dog's coat for a while.

4. 1 tsp liquid handsoap or dishwashing liquid + 1 qt hydrogen peroxide + ½ cup baking soda

Snake Bites: These are very serious! Take your pet to the veterinarian immediately and, if you can identify the type of snake, be sure to tell him or her. Your vet can treat your pet with IVs, antivenin (within 4 hours after the bite), antibiotics or non-steroidal anti-inflammatory drugs (during the first 24 hours). Your pet needs to be observed for at least 12 hours.

Snakes leave small puncture wounds. There may be some bruising or bleeding and painful swelling. Other symptoms include nausea, vomiting, weakness, and shock.

Spider Bites: If you suspect your pet has been bitten by a spider, check for visible blisters, which are often but not always present. Your pet may react to the venom in two to six hours. Take your pet to the veterinarian's office if he exhibits the following symptoms: increased heart rate, paralysis, severe abdominal pain, drooling, cramping of the back and chest (signs of a black widow bite); vomiting, weakness, seizures, and pain (signs of a brown recluse bite). Spider bites can be very serious, leading to respiratory or cardiovascular collapse and death.

If you see and can safely contain the spider that bit your pet, take it to the veternarian's office for identification.

Toxins in the Yard and Home

Medications: Keep all medications stored away from pets. They are so curious and will get into everything they can literally get their paws on! Remind house guests also to keep their medications in a safe place. If you have any questions, contact your local poison control or the **American Association of Poison Control Centers at 1-800-222-1222.**

Pesticides: Pesticides are created for one purpose—to kill pests! This is why you must use them very carefully around your home. Be sure to choose the correct pesticide for your job. According to the American Association of Poison Control Centers, "When buying pesticides carefully follow all instructions on the container. Wear protective clothing, mask and eye protection when spraying. Choose a calm, wind-free day." You do not want the mist to land on yourself or any other part of the yard where you do not want pesticides applied, like near plants or gardens.

When you're finished using pesticides, be sure to clean your hands, face and clothes. Store them in a safe place away from pets and children and away from food. Do not transfer pesticides from one container to another; they must also be disposed of properly.

Keep in mind, vinegar is an alternative to other harmful weed killers. Any type of vinegar can be used. This works best when temperatures are above 70 degrees. You may have to pull your weeds first and then spray to prevent future weeds. Note that vinegar will kill all plants as well as sod, so be careful where you spray it!

If you find bugs on your vegetable plants, try using soap and water to get rid of them. Depending on the size of your garden, you can either use a spray bottle with two tablespoons of dishwashing soap with water or two tablespoons of dishwashing soap in a garden sprayer that attaches to your garden hose. Or talk to your nursery professional about organic options to use on your vegetable garden.

During the Winter & Holidays

Winter weather and holidays both pose additional concerns with pet safety. Here are some tips to keep you mindful of extra precautions.

* Holiday lights can entice all kinds of pets; little do they know how dangerous it is to chew on electrical cords. Keep your precious pets away so they don't get electrocuted!

* Chocolate candy under the tree is easy for dogs to smell. They will eat the package as well as the candy. Remember, just one ounce of baking chocolate or cocoa powder is toxic. Also toxic to dogs: macadamia nuts and diabetic Sorbitol candy.

* All those glittering ornaments and ribbons can also be hazardous to curious pets. Glass bulbs can shatter and tinsel can get stuck inside your pet's body. Make sure to hang all these tempting items high on the tree, away from your pet's reach. Even your

presents with the beautifully decorated yarns and ribbons can cause your pets harm.

* Keep holiday plants such as holly and mistletoe away from your pets' reach. Many holiday plants including poinsettias are extremely poisonous when eaten.

* Christmas tree water and pine needles can cause upset stomachs. Don't let your pet drink that water. And remember that some trees are chemically treated, making the needles quite toxic.

* Holiday guests often inadvertently leave the door open. This can lead to unexpected escapes. Be sure your pets have identification on them, and have a recent photo of your pet, just in case. Better yet, before your guests arrive, place your pets in a secure environment; holiday visits by strange humans can be very stressful on them.

* Knock hard on the hood of your car or honk the horn before starting the engine. Many outdoor cats or other critters seek the warmth from your car engine during the cold winter months.

* Antifreeze can kill animals! Keep all antifreeze containers away from your pets. For some reason, animals seem to like the taste and smell of it; they have no idea that they are drinking a fatal cocktail. Make sure to clean up any spills at once because even the smallest amount can kill them.

* Remember that dogs can get dehydrated quickly. If left outdoors with the correct shelter from the sun, wind, rain, and snow, dogs will still always need water. Ice and snow are not substitutes for liquid water. Get a heated source or replace water at least twice a day.

* Remove any ice melt from your pets' paws and coat. The synthetic ice melt can cause severe irritation to your pet.

TAILWAGGIN' TIPS

These snacks are no treat!

Even though I might beg for the **bones** from the holiday turkey or ham, just say "no!" The smaller bones can chip and lodge in my throat, stomach, or intestinal tract. This obstruction can lead to a life-threatening condition, not to mention a large financial burden if surgery is required. No fun for either of us...

Chocolate is also a major no-no—it can even be fatal. Make sure you put the platters of yummies away after your parties or I just might help myself. Think it's safely wrapped under the tree? Ah, my nose should not be underestimated!

First Aid

In the event of an emergency, be sure to have these items on hand:
- Hydrogen peroxide (3%) to induce vomiting
- A muzzle to prevent your pet from hurting you while he is in pain or nervously excited
- Gauze for wounds (or to use as a muzzle, if not applied too tightly)
- Pet carrier to transport your injured animal to the veterinarian
- Rubber gloves to protect yourself while bathing your pet
- Canned food can be used to make a meatball for giving pills to a dog. Peanut butter or cheese can also be used.

Uh, Oh…Poisonous Plants!

According to Rocky Mountain Poison Control, poisonings from eating plants are common in children under the age of 5 and pets of all ages. Be sure to educate yourself with the information provided here and with the help of professionals at your local landscape center before choosing plants for your home and garden. By knowing what to select and where to plant, you can greatly reduce the potential risks.

Many plants appear beautiful but can cause serious problems to your pet. These plants create a toxic reaction in pets at different quantities; they're not all poisonous when ingested at the same rate. A plant's level of toxicity can be different at different times of the year, depending on whether they are in dormancy, blooming, in a drought, established, healthy, or withering.

Symptoms from plant poisonings vary greatly; some plants may cause skin irritation, mouth irritation, nausea, vomiting or more serious effects. If you suspect your Backyard Barney has gotten into a poisonous plant, do act quickly but don't panic! Collect evidence of the type of plant he ate, if at all possible (whether it's a branch that's noticeably chewed on or pieces of the plant are in his stools or vomit), and take him to the veterinarian as quickly as possible. Even if it's precautionary, it's better to be safe than sorry where potentially toxic plants are concerned.

Poisonous Plants Commonly Used in Landscaping

Botanical Name	Common Name
Abrus precatorius	Jequirity Bean, Rosary Bean, Precatory Bean

Actonitum napellus	Monkshood, Aconite
Aesulus Species	Horse-Chestnut, Buckeye
Apocynum cannabinum	Dogbane, Indian Hemp
Arisaema triphyllum	Jack-in-the-pulpit
Asparagus officinalis	Asparagus
Atropa belladonna	Belladonna, Deadly Nightshade
Buxus semperivirens	Boxwood, Common box
Cestrum Nocturnum	Night Blooming Jessamine
Ciscuta Species	Water Hemlock
Cochicum autumnale	Autumn crocus
Conium Maculatum	Poison Hemlock
Convallaria majalis	Lily-of-the-Valley
Datura stramonium	Jimson weed
Delphinium species	Larkspur, Delphinium
Dieffenbachia species	Dumbcane, Dieffenbachia
Digitalis purpurea	Foxglove
Euphorbia marginata	Snow-on-the-mountain
Euphorbia pulcherrima	Poinsettia
Euphoribia tirucalli	Pencil tree
Glechoma hederacea	Ground Ivy
Nepeta hederacea	Gill-over-the-ground
Glymnocladus dioica	Kentucky Coffee Tree
Hendera helix	English Ivy
Hyacinthus orientalis	Hyacinth
Hydrangea species	Hydrangea
Hyoscyamus niger	Poison tobacco, Black Henbane
Ipomoea tricolor	Morning Glory
Iris Species	Iris
Juniperus virginiana	Juniper
Laburum anagyroides	Golden Chain tree, Laburnum
Ligustrum vulgare	Privet
Mirabilis jalapa	Four-o-clocks
Mushrooms	Mushroom
Narcissus species	Daffodil, Jonquil, Narcissus
Philodendron species	Filodendros
Phoradendron flavescens	Mistletoe
Prunus virginiana	Chokecherry
Quercus species	Oak
Rhamnus cathartica	Buckthorn
Rhus radicans	Poison Ivy
Rhus vernix	Poison Sumac

Robinia pseudoacacia	Black Locust
Sambucus species	Elder, Elderberry
Solanum Pseudocapsicum	Jerusalem Cherry
Solanum dulcamara	European Bittersweet
Solanum nigrum	Deadly Nightshade
Symphoricaros alba	Snowberry
Symplocarpus foetidus	Skunk Cabbage
Taxus species	Yew
Thevetia peruviana	Be-still-tree
Veratrum viride	Fallse Hellebore, Hellebore, Indian Poke

Poisonous Plants commonly used in the Rocky Mountain Region: Montana, North Dakota, South Dakota, Wyoming, Utah, Colorado

Anthurium species	Anthurium, Tailflower
Aphelandra squarrosa	Aphelandra
Begonia species	Begonias
Brassaia Actinophylla	Schefflera
Chamaedorea elegans	Parlor palm
Chlorophytum comosum variegatum	Spider plant
Coleus blumei	Coleus
Crassula argentea	Jade Plant
Ficus elastica	Rubber Tree
Gynura aurantiaca	Velvet, Purple Passion
Helxine soleirolii	Baby Tears
Hemoerocallis lilioasphodelus	Yellow Day-Lily
Hoya Carnosa	Hoya
Impatiens species	Patient Lucy, Impatiens
Iresine species	Blood-leaf
Maranta Leuconeura (Kerchoveana/Erythoroneura)	Prayer Plant
Nephrolepis exaltata	Boston Fern
Peperomia	Emerald Ripple, Peperomia, Peperomia
Pilea cadierei	Aluminum Plant
Pilea nummularifolia	Creeping Charlie
Plectranthus australis	Swedish Ivy
Saintpaulia ionantha	African Violets
Scheffler actinophylla	Schefflera
Zygocatcus species	Christmas cactussa

For a more complete list, click on the Poisonous Plants tab on my Web site: www.pawfriendlylandscapes.com.

If you already have a garden with these plants and do not want to remove them, you can create barriers to prevent your Backyard Barney from playing around them. For instance, installing large cobble (especially if your dog is small or medium size) will prevent him from going into the garden. Or creating a barrier, such as an attractive fence, will also prevent him from getting into the garden.

IN CASE OF EMERGENCY, call your local poison center immediately. The Poison Center can tell you over the phone if your animal should see a veterinarian.

The good news is that most dogs do not like the taste of toxic plants so they do not eat the quantities required to create a toxic reaction. Young dogs, however, tend to be curious and will chew or carry just about anything, whether it tastes good or not!

Pet Poison Safety "Do's and Don'ts" from the Poison Control Center

DO'S:

These poison safety tips apply to children as well as pets.

Call your family doctor or dial 911 if you believe your child has been exposed to poison. |

1. Know the botanical names of plants and trees in your home and yard; keep poisonous varieties from pets.
2. Replace wood mulch with rock mulch if you notice your pet chewing or eating the wood mulch.
3. Pay close attention to your pet if a stomach virus or parasite appears to be affecting him; ill pets are more likely to ingest unusual things in an attempt to calm their stomachs.
4. Keep cleaners, bug sprays, windshield washer fluid, oil, paint, antifreeze, medicines, and other harmful products out of your pet's environment. If possible, keep the products locked up. Always keep them in their original containers.
5. Only feed pet food to your pet. Just one ounce of chocolate can kill your dog! High fat foods can cause indigestion as well as damage to the pancreas. Examples of fatty foods are peanuts, whole milk, ground beef, bacon, ham and giblets, dark meat, and skin from poultry. Also, there have been reports of dogs suffering from kidney failure after eating large amounts of grapes or raisins.
6. When discarding household products, rinse containers and put them in a covered trash can that is inaccessible to your pets.

7. Keep your pets out of the area when using insecticides and pesticides; use caution in placement of mousetraps.
8. Keep painted surfaces in good condition.
9. Store bulbs and seeds out of reach of pets.

DON'TS:

1. Don't store potentially toxic products near your pet's food.
2. Don't give human medicine to your pet unless a veterinarian says it's OK.
3. Don't leave household products and medicines unattended. If interrupted while using them, put them away so your pet can't get into them.
4. Don't put gasoline, bug spray, antifreeze, or cleaning supplies in soft-drink bottles, cups or bowls that could attract pets.
5. Never assume a plant is not poisonous because birds or other wildlife eat it—this includes berries and mushrooms.
6. Do not rely on cooking to destroy toxic chemicals in plants.
7. Don't use rodent killers in or near your home; pets can be poisoned if they eat carcasses of rodents killed in this way.

Pets Can Get Into Things at Any Age!

Animals age 0 to 8 weeks
- ◆ Start to explore home and yard
- ◆ Learn about their environment by putting things in their mouths
- ◆ Chew on things because they are teething

Animals age 9 weeks to 2 years
- ◆ Curiosity is high; most at risk of being poisoned
- ◆ May wander from home, especially if not spayed or neutered

Animals age 25 months and up
- ◆ Know where to find food and garbage; may stumble across toxic items
- ◆ Overweight pets may eat potentially toxic items

TAILWAGGIN' TIPS

I might like to eat a lot, but that doesn't mean I should. Obesity causes similar problems in pets as it does in humans (decreased mobility, heart and lung problems, reduced efficiency of pancreas) as well as bloated and twisted stomachs.

Seasonal Dangers

Spring and Summer Dangers
- ◆ Pesticides
- ◆ Fertilizers
- ◆ Antifreeze drained from cars and poured in the street or stored improperly
- ◆ Charcoal lighter fluid
- ◆ Outdoor plants and mushrooms
- ◆ Snake, spider and insect bites and stings
- ◆ Ticks

Fall and Winter Dangers
- ◆ Antifreeze (tastes sweet; even a small amount can kill a pet in 18 hours)
- ◆ Dehydration (ice and snow are not substitutes for liquid water; get a heated source or replace water at least twice a day)
- ◆ Carbon monoxide
- ◆ Black widow spider bites
- ◆ Plants and autumn berries
- ◆ Holly, mistletoe, glass ornaments, tinsel, ribbon and other holiday decorations
- ◆ Chocolate and other holiday foods

"Just In Case" Remedies

If your pet...

Breathes poison: immediately get the animal to fresh air; avoid breathing fumes; open doors and windows wide.

Gets poison on the skin: flood skin with water for 10 minutes; then wash gently with soap and water, and rinse.

Gets poison in the eye: flood the eye with lukewarm (not hot) water poured from a large glass, 2 or 3 inches from the eye. Repeat for 15 minutes. Do not force the eyelid open.

Swallows medicines: do not give pet anything until you talk with the poison center or your veterinarian.

Swallows chemicals or household products: unless your pet has passed out or cannot swallow, give water right away.

Resources

Association of Occupational and Environmental Clinics (AOEC)
1-202-347-4976
www.aoec.org

Agency for Toxic Substance Disease Registry (ATSDR)
1-888-42-ATSDR
www.atsdr.cdc.gov

Environmental Protection Agency (EPA)
www.epa.gov

Consumer Product Safety Commission
1-800-638-CPSC
www.cpsc.gov

National Jewish Lung Line
1-800-222-LUNG

National Poison Control Centers Line
1-800-222-1222

ASPCA Animal Poison Control Center
1-800-426-4435

Now that you know how to prevent poisons and you're educated on particular plants that can cause a toxic reaction, always remember: if you live in a cold climate, do not eat yellow snow!

Chapter 6: Our Feline Friends

Perhaps your backyard dilemmas are of the feline variety. Generally the problem is this: you have an indoor cat that wants "out." And she complains rather loudly until you give in. But we all know that cats can be in serious danger if they leave the house, whether from other animals or vehicles. Sometimes they venture out and can't find their way home. Believe it or not, there are solutions.

Cat Enclosures

John Kuepper of Denver, Colorado, was determined to find a safe way for his cats to enjoy the outdoors after his loving cat Clarence was attacked by a dog while sitting in the driveway. His desire to protect the feline critters he adored made him an observer of cats' behavior and eventually his company, Cat-Man-Do, was created.

John creates cat enclosure systems as well as indoor/outdoor cat perches, catwalks, litter box ventilation systems (great for multi-cat households), ramps and steps for aging pets, "mouse" holes (which are cat-size holes for interior doors), and pet doors. He has been perfecting his cat containment techniques for almost a decade.

> Just like their larger cousins, domestic cats run on instinct and they need to roam and explore their territory. The trick is to control the size of that territory.

Cats are constantly exploring, looking, and calculating to determine if they can get to this perch or fit through that opening; discovering these routes *before they do* and finding a way to obstruct the routes is the key to keeping your cats at home.

Cats have amazing personalities: some adventurous and downright conniving, some laidback, and some downright lazy. In general, it would seem that cats are constantly trying to conserve energy; if they have to put too much effort into escaping, they won't likely bother. Simply making escape inconvenient can be very effective for deterring some cats. Of course some cats will attempt seemingly impossible things to get out and, if successful, they will perfect this action until it seems effortless—unless the escape route is located and blocked. On the other extreme, many cats are just happy to lounge outside in the sun undisturbed. Your cat could be a combination of any of these "personality types," as described by John.

The trouble with Simon

We adopted Simon as a tiny kitten; he grew into what we lovingly called the "Monster," ultimately peaking at 18 pounds. Even though Simon grew up with access to a secured backyard, he *had* to get out and explore and expand his domain. Eventually he started running and jumping over a brick wall onto our 8-foot-tall, flat-roofed garage. He'd hang out up there for a bit and then eventually disappear into the alley or jump over the fence onto our neighbor's shed.

The solution was to let Simon (and our other cats) onto our garage by way of a ramp system and then simply prevent him from jumping off. Now they all sit up there and look at the world from the safety of their very own sundeck.

The Trouble with Faye

Faye loves to be outside and howls to get what she wants; from a distance it sounds like a crying baby. Faye has the run of the entire house *and* the entire backyard, but when people are in the front yard, she howls to be with them. A leash was not the answer—too cumbersome.

The solution was to enclose a small portion of the front porch and let Faye have access with a cat door installed in a window. Faye can now sit on the front porch whenever she wants; she is happy and the neighbors are no longer asking, "Do you hear a baby crying?"

The Trouble with Lucy

Lucy enjoys being outside but *only* if she knows she can go back inside anytime she wants, like at the drop of a leaf, for instance, or if a bird chirps too loudly. Lucy, it seemed, would've preferred the screen door be simply propped open for her at all times.

The solution was to install a pet door so Lucy could have unlimited access to the backyard—and the family's screen door has returned to its regular duty.

John has playfully nicknamed his enclosure system the Penitentiary®. He also creates ramps, low-profile security fences, balcony enclosures, cat doors, tunnels, perches, you name it!

Of course, if you're a die-hard do-it-yourselfer, you can follow John's lead and create a custom system for your own cat or cats—keeping them entertained and safe using lattice, welded wire, and other materials from your local hardware store. Feel free to contact John at www.catman-do.com.

The Purrfect Backyard

Certain plant material is great for cats. Catnip is cheap and very easy to grow. When I'm creating a cat-friendly yard, I always include catnip, but I do like to warn people: stay on top of it, or it will spread like wildfire! All your neighbor cats will visit and your place will become a real "cat house"— "cat bar" and all!

One way to keep catnip under control is to grow it indoors in a special window-sill herb garden. Since it is an herb, it needs a lot of sun. Cats also like to lay in sunny areas, so after they're done grazing, they can take a catnap, literally! If you must have catnip outdoors, a trick to keep it from spreading is to grow it in pots outside. In zones where we have pretty harsh winters, plants in containers tend not to "overwinter" (survive the winter) so you may have to buy more catnip the following year—much like an annual.

Another favorite plant for cats is grass. They love to roll and play in grass—they also love to eat it!—so always have a safe place for them to relax and enjoy their own little spot of lawn. Grass can be grown indoors in containers as well. It is very easy to grow, so even a beginner or someone with a not-so-green thumb can have plenty of success. Besides being desirable for cats, it is very attractive and can add an interesting texture when displayed in decorative pots in your home. One word of caution: the blades will be noticeably chewed on by your cat. Artificial grass and silk plants, on the other hand, can be harmful to your kitty, causing an obstruction if swallowed. (Cats cannot spit things out; their tongues have little spikes pointing down their throats. So if something gets in a cat's mouth, it probably will go down.)

If there's one surefire way to please your cats, it is to make sure they have a nice sunny place to nap. Since they only get about 23 hours of sleep per day, it's best to include some places for them to lounge when they're in their yard! We've discovered cats love to sit on or next to boulders; the bigger and flatter the face of the boulder, the happier they are while they bask in the sun.

One final suggestion I must add: if you do have outdoor cats, it's best not to install any type of bird feeders or bird baths. As you might imagine, this is very cruel and unfair to the birds. However, if your cats are indoors or in an enclosure, you can create a beautiful bird and butterfly sanctuary so they can sit in their favorite window and watch them fly back and forth between naps!   Your kitty will enjoy viewing birds from indoors or a place where the birds are protected from the cat's instinct:

Bird and Butterfly-attracting Perennials:
Asters
Avens
Beard Tongue
Bee Balm
Black-eyed Susan
Blanket Flower
Bush Cinquefolia
Butterfly Weed
Catmint
Clary Sage
Common Sneezeweek
Coneflower
Cosmos
Gaillardia
Lilac
Cupid Dart
Desert Paper Flower
Double Bubble Mint
Dragonhead
Dwarf Pincushion
False Sunflower
Fennel
Foxglove
Garden Lily
Garden Sage
Garlic Chives
Gayfeather
Globe Thistle
Goldenrod
Great Lobelia
Hardy Cactus
Hollyhock
Hollyhock Mallow

Hyssop
Inula
Jacob's Ladder
Jupiter's Beard
Knautia
Lobelia
Maltese Cross
Marigold
Ornamental Thistles
Meadow Rue
Mexican Evening Primrose
Mint
Money Plant
Mullein
Native Four O'Clocks
NY Ironweed
Obedient Plant
Ornamental Oregano
Parsley
Perennial Verbena
Pincushion
Pinks Dianthus
Plumbago
Plume Poppy
Poppy
Poppy Mallow
Rabbitbrush
Primrose
Salvia
Spike Speedwell
Strawberry
Sunflower
Sweet Pea
Verbena
Zinnias
Butterfly Bush
Butterfly Plant
Tall Sedum
Thyme
Trumpet Vine
Valerian

Butterfly and Bird-Attracting Trees and Shrubs:

All fruit trees
Hackberry
Hawthorn
Crabapples
Chokecherry
Hornbeam
Cherry Plum
Mountain Ash
Serviceberry
Yucca
Coralberry
Cotoneaster
Golden Currant
Chokeberry
Butterfly Bush
Thimbleberry
Silver Buffaloberry
American Elder
Viburnum
Western Sandcherry
Arnold Red Honeysuckle
American Plum
Maiden/Plume Grass

TRAINING TIPS: Dr. Spurling

Citrus peelings (oranges, grapefruit) or mothballs scattered in a garden deter cats from eliminating in those areas. (Caution: Some dogs eat mothballs, so only use if your Barney doesn't eat them!)

Chapter 7: Quick Landscape Tips for Everyone
with or without pets…

◆ When buying edging or any landscape material, always add 10 percent more. You'll be glad you have the extra for any needed cuts, overlapping, or "goofs" (yep, they happen to us all). So for example, if your linear footage is 80 feet, add 10 percent, or 8 feet of edging. You'll actually need to buy 90 feet, since edging is sold in 10-foot increments. Remember to buy six pins per 10 feet of edging as well.

◆ Since our yards have so many lines (our fences, homes and buildings), it's best to create landscapes using soft, meandering curves. This not only softens the look of your yard but also creates interesting shapes in your yard, whether for grass, berms or garden areas. It is much more visually appealing.

◆ Take a lot of notes; you can never have too many job notes. Always know your square footage prior to calling or visiting any nursery or bulk material store. The first question the supplier will ask is, "What is your square footage?" They'll do the conversions.

◆ Stagger your plants; do not install the plants in a straight row (like crops). They will fill in quicker and have a nicer look.

◆ Always plant using groupings of odd numbers to avoid a choppy look. Single plants work well as accents if they can "stand alone," like ornamental grasses or dwarf spruces, such as Glauca Globosa, R.H. Montgomery, etc.

FROM THE TRENCHES

Matt installed edging between his concrete walkway and shrub garden to keep his rock mulch from falling on the sidewalk. He wanted to prevent the rock from migrating to the sidewalk since neighbor kids would kick and throw the rock as they walked to and from school everyday. Luckily, Matt was in good company. This is such a common problem I see when homeowners install any type of mulch near a walkway.

Our remedy: At the time of the installation of the mulch, Matt should have *removed* at least three inches of dirt since he was going to *add* two to three inches of rock mulch. In this situation, the concrete should be used as the edger and the rock mulch (or wood mulch) should be flush with the concrete. Installing edging in this situation is superfluous.

◆ If you live in a climate with harsh winters, consider a winter palette. Since the growing season is so short, use evergreens, red or yellow twig dogwoods, barberries (doggie deterrent), blue mist spirea (which attracts bees, so do not plant near dog runs), and bulk material such as boulders or dry cobble bed.

◆ When you have a large scale of rock mulch or sod, be sure to incorporate accents, such as dry cobble beds, berms, or different mulch textures throughout the garden area.

◆ Do you want to make your garden "pop"? Incorporate complimentary colors. These colors are opposite on the color wheel, so when you plant them together, they create energy! The three complementary colors are: 1) green/red—for a winter palette use doggie-deterrent green evergreens (Calgary, Buffalo, Sea Green, Scandia, Tammy, Arcadia, Greenmound) with Red Barberries and Red Twig Dogwoods; 2) yellow/purple—for a winter palette, install doggie-deterrent blue junipers, which turn purple in the winter (Wichita Blue, Dwarf forms of Spruces, such as Glauca Globosa, Broadmoor, Wiltoni, Hughes, Blue Chip, Bar Harbor) next to Yellow Twig Dogwoods; 3) orange/blue—for a fall palette use blue junipers next to Peking Cotoneaster, Legacy Maple, or doggie-deterrent Pyracatha for its orange berries.

◆ Remember, your front door is your focal point—design your front yard so the eye is led to your door. Install tall plants at the outskirts of your yard and smaller ones toward the door. This will lead the eye toward the door.

◆ Be sure to plant large shade and evergreen trees 15 feet from your house or any structure since trees grow into homes. If you don't have a large yard, then use ornamental trees like Crabapples, Hawthorns or Upright Junipers, since they don't get very big.

Coverage Chart for Bulk Material

Landscape Fabric	=	square footage
$\frac{3}{4}$-inch Rock Mulch	=	1 ton covers 105 square feet (3 inches deep)
Pea Gravel	=	1 ton covers 50 square feet (4 inches deep)
2-4-inch Cobblestone	=	1 ton covers 60 square feet
5-12-inch Cobblestone	=	1 ton covers 30 square feet

*Your measurements will always be the variable. Take your square footage and divide any of these constants, per your needs. For example: I have 90 square feet of a new doggie area (plus 10 percent for incidentals, so 99 or 100 square feet). I need pea gravel and roll-top edging. I will divide my 100 by 50 (for pea gravel) = 2 tons of pea gravel. My length is 9 x 10 feet, so I will need two pieces of 10-foot edging. Since I like to buy a little more for incidentals, I would actually buy three pieces. I also need edging pins: six per 10 feet, or approximately 18 pins, to be prepared. Viola! You're ready!

Thank you so much, friends, for allowing us to show you how you and your best friend can live harmoniously. There is absolutely no need to relinquish your dog to a shelter for "destructive" behavior in the backyard. There are so many ways to deter him from destroying your backyard. We hope you will enjoy and benefit from these ideas, and find them easy and effective to use.

Have suggestions based on your own Backyard Barney discoveries? Please email them to: Info@pawfriendlylandscapes.com

Have fun...and get dirty!

Pawfriendly Landscapes

How to share the turf when your "backyard belongs to Barney"

by Elizabeth Bublitz

I.S.B.N. 1-59879-525-2

Available Online at:

www.authorstobelievein.com

By Phone Toll Free at:

1-877-843-1007